Walter Foster

W9-CUX-997

HOW TO DRAW
GARFIELD
AND FRIENDS

BY JIM DAVIS

Step-by-Step Drawing Illustrations by Ron Zalme • Text by Michael Teitelbaum, Ron Zalme & Scott Nickel
Designed by Shelley Baugh • Project Editor: Rebecca J. Razo

TOOLS AND MATERIALS

Before you begin your drawing, you will need to gather a few simple tools. Start with a regular pencil so you can easily erase any mistakes. Make sure to have an eraser and a pencil sharpener, too! When you are finished drawing, use colored pencils, markers, or crayons to bring your characters to life!

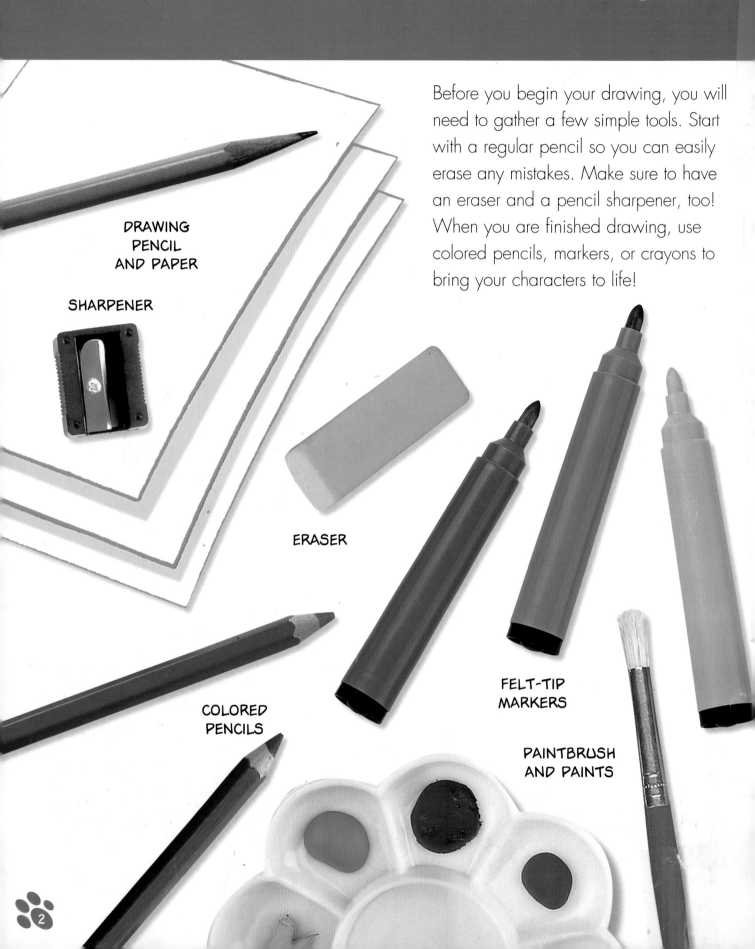

DRAWING
PENCIL
AND PAPER

SHARPENER

ERASER

COLORED
PENCILS

FELT-TIP
MARKERS

PAINTBRUSH
AND PAINTS

GETTING STARTED

By following these simple steps, you'll be drawing Garfield and his friends in no time!

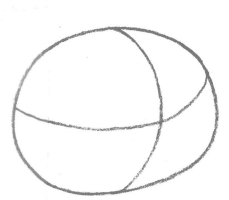

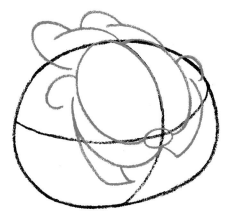

1. FIRST DRAW THE BASIC SHAPES IN THE MIDDLE OF THE PAPER SO YOU DON'T RUN OUT OF ROOM.

2. EACH NEW STEP IS SHOWN IN BLUE, SO JUST DRAW ALL THE BLUE LINES THAT YOU SEE.

3. CONTINUE TO FOLLOW THE BLUE LINES TO ADD THE DETAILS.

4. CLEAN UP THE SKETCHY PENCIL LINES WITH AN ERASER AND ADD THE FINAL STRIPES AND DOTS.

5. ADD VIVID COLORS TO BRING YOUR DRAWING TO LIFE ON PAPER!

GARFIELD'S HEAD

Hey, future cartoonists of the world! Before you begin drawing, here are a couple of quick tips: 1) Draw lightly as you sketch; you'll have a plenty of time to darken your lines and fill in the details as you finish your drawing. 2) Stay loose (like a goose!). Let your hand and arm move freely. Don't tighten up or hold your pencil in a "death grip." Relax! Drawing, like eating, should be a fun activity. 3) Don't be afraid to make a mistake—that's why they invented erasers! 4) Finally, remember that the poses in this book are guides to help you understand how to draw me and my friends by building on basic shapes. The more you practice drawing, the better you'll get. Soon you'll be able to make up your own poses, situations, and stories (just make sure you draw lots of food for me to eat!).

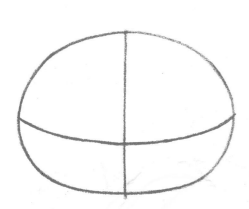

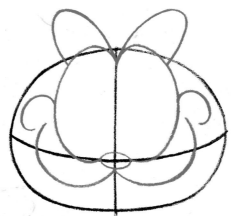

1. START WITH A BASIC OVAL SHAPE— LIKE A WATERMELON (YUM!). DRAW A STRAIGHT LINE DIVIDING THE OVAL IN HALF VERTICALLY. THEN DRAW A HORIZONTAL LINE 1/4 OF THE WAY UP FROM THE BOTTOM OF THE OVAL. CURVE THIS LINE SO IT APPEARS TO BE GOING AROUND THE OVAL.

2. DRAW A SMALL CIRCLE FOR GARFIELD'S NOSE RIGHT WHERE THE VERTICAL AND HORIZONTAL LINES CROSS. ADD EARS. THEN DRAW TWO LARGE OVALS FOR HIS EYES (ALSO KNOWN AS "PASTA SPOTTERS"). GIVE HIM A NICE BIG SMILE. THE ENDS OF THE SMILE SHOULD REACH HALFWAY UP HIS EYE OVALS.

3. COMPLETE THE EARS AND ADD ONE EXTRA LINE TO GIVE GARFIELD HIS FAMOUS DOUBLE CHIN. NOW ADD HIS WHISKERS, EYELIDS, AND TWO DOTS FOR HIS EYES.

4. CLEAN UP THE SKETCHY PENCIL LINES WITH AN ERASER, AND ADD THE FINAL STRIPES AND DOTS. PRESTO! YOU'VE COMPLETED GARFIELD'S HEAD. BEHOLD THE HUNGRIEST CAT IN HISTORY!

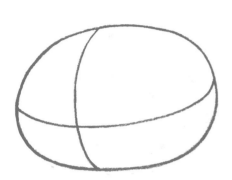

1. JUST AS WITH THE FRONT VIEW, START WITH A LARGE OVAL AND ADD THE HORIZONTAL AND VERTICAL LINES, ONLY THIS TIME PLACE THE VERTICAL LINE OFF-CENTER (TOWARD THE SIDE YOU WANT GARFIELD TO FACE. CURVE THE LINE SO IT APPEARS TO BE GOING AROUND THE OVAL.

2. ADD THE EYE OVALS, EARS, NOSE, AND MOUTH AS BEFORE, ONLY THIS TIME NOTICE THAT THE EARS BOTH ANGLE TOWARD THE SIDE YOU WANT GARFIELD TO FACE.

3. FILL OUT GARFIELD'S FACE AND NOTE HOW THE CHIN AND CHEEK LINES OVERLAP IN THE SAME DIRECTION.

4. CLEAN UP THE SKETCHY PENCIL LINES WITH AN ERASER, AND ADD THE FINAL STRIPES AND DOTS. NOTICE THAT YOU SEE MORE STRIPES ON THE SIDE OF THE HEAD THAT'S TURNED TOWARD YOU.

I THINK I'LL TAKE A NAP

JIM DAVIS 8-27

THEN DOZE AWHILE...AND THEN TOP IT ALL OFF WITH A NICE SNOOZE

REMEMBER, KIDS, FOR WELL-BALANCED REST, YOU MUST HAVE SOMETHING FROM THE THREE BASIC SLEEP GROUPS EACH DAY

Now that you've learned how to draw Garfield's head, let's give the feisty fat cat some facial expressions: 1) Keep ovals somewhat flattened on bottom. 2) Lips thicken at ends. 3) Note extra height of head for the happy and excited (in other words, hungry) look. Also, the teeth are evenly spaced squares extending out from both sides of the center of the smile. 4) Nose should be slightly off-center of the crossing horizontal and vertical lines in the three-quarter views.

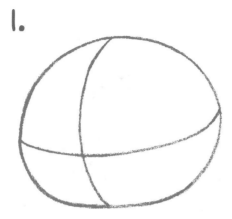

1.

KEEP OVALS SOMEWHAT FLATTENED ON BOTTOM.

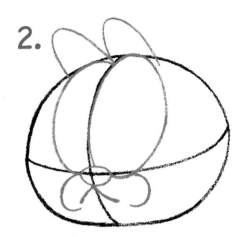

2.

3.

LIPS THICKEN AT ENDS.

4.

6

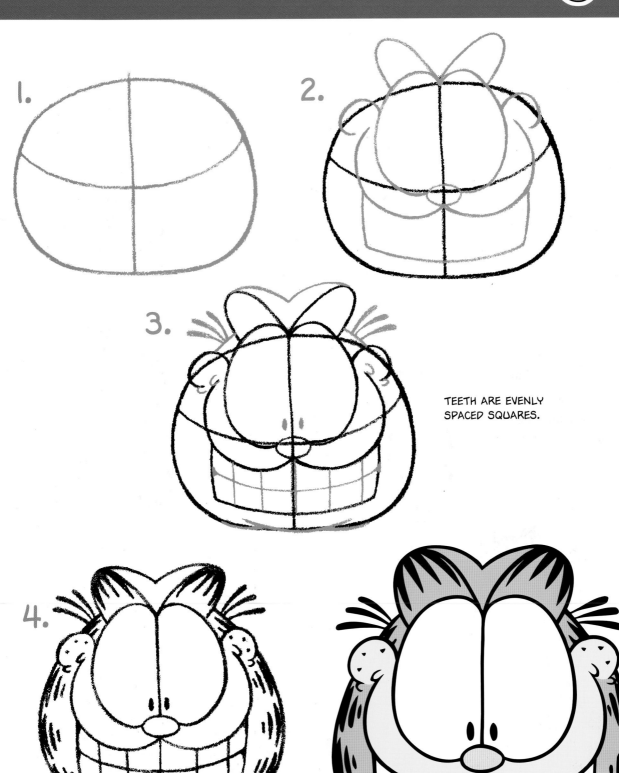

1.

2.

3.

TEETH ARE EVENLY
SPACED SQUARES.

4.

NOTE EXTRA HEIGHT OF HEAD FOR
THAT HAPPY OR EXCITED LOOK.

SITTING

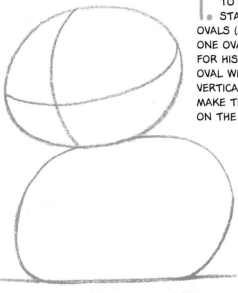

1. TO SHOW GARFIELD'S BODY, START WITH TWO LARGE OVALS (AND LOTS OF PAPER)— ONE OVAL FOR HIS HEAD, ONE FOR HIS BODY. DIVIDE THE HEAD OVAL WITH HORIZONTAL AND VERTICAL LINES AS BEFORE. MAKE THE BODY OVAL FLAT ON THE BOTTOM.

2. PLACE CIRCLES ALONG THE BOTTOM LINE OF THE BODY OVAL TO POSITION THE FEET AND TAIL. ADD THE EYE OVALS, EARS, NOSE, AND MOUTH.

STANDING

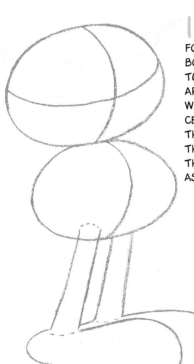

1. AGAIN, USE TWO OVALS FOR THE HEAD AND BODY. GARFIELD'S TUBE-SHAPED LEGS ARE QUITE LONG WHEN HE'S STANDING. CENTER THEM UNDER THE BODY OVAL SO THEY LOOK BALANCED. THEN ADD HIS FEET AS SHOWN.

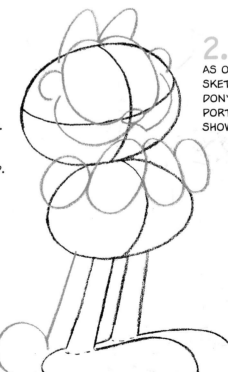

2. IT'S EASIER TO THINK OF GARFIELD'S HANDS AS ONE ENTIRE SHAPE WHEN SKETCHING, SO THE FINGERS DON'T GET OUT OF PRO- PORTION. DRAW THESE AS SHOWN; THEN ADD HIS TAIL.

8

3. FILL IN THE PAWS AND ROUND OUT THE BODY TO GIVE GARFIELD HIS FAMOUS PEAR SHAPE (ALTHOUGH HE GOT IT MORE FROM EATING FRIED FOOD THAN FROM FRUIT). FILL IN FACIAL DETAILS AS BEFORE.

4. CLEAN UP THE SKETCH LINES AND FINISH YOUR DRAWING BY ADDING GARFIELD'S STRIPES.

3. NOW IT'S TIME TO FILL IN THE DETAILS OF HIS FINGERS AND TOES. ALSO NOTICE HOW THE SHAPE OF HIS HEEL CHANGES.

4. DRAW THE FINAL DETAILS. DID YOU REMEMBER TO ADD THE SHADOWS AT THE TOP OF GARFIELD'S REAR LEG AND TAIL?

Now that you've learned how to draw Garfield's body, let's put him in some common poses:

SLEEPING

1.

SCRUNCH UP THE BODY OVAL TO GIVE GARFIELD
A COZY LOOK WHILE HE'S SLEEPING.

2.

WALKING

1. WHEN HIS
FEET, HANDS,
OR TAIL GO
BEHIND HIS BODY,
IT GIVES YOUR
DRAWING A 3-D
FEELING.

2. A SMOOTH
CURVE TO THE
TAIL GIVES THE FAT
CAT THE LOOK OF
LIVELY ACTION.

RUNNING

1.

2.

TRY THESE:

3.

3.

3.

THE TINIER THE
PUPILS, THE MORE
GARFIELD WILL
LOOK FRIGHTENED
OR SURPRISED.

FRONT VIEW

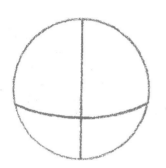

1. TO DRAW A FRONT VIEW, START WITH A CIRCLE. THEN DIVIDE IT WITH HORIZONTAL AND VERTICAL LINES AS SHOWN.

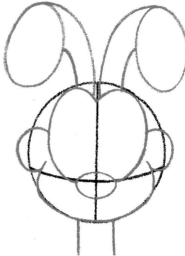

2. CENTER THE NOSE, ADD THE EYES AND EARS, AND CHANGE THE FACE SHAPE AS SHOWN. NOTE HOW THE CHEEKS LINE UP ON THE HORIZONTAL LINE.

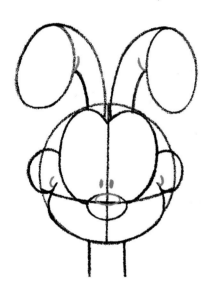

3. ODIE'S EARS SHOULD BE PERKY. THE OVAL SHAPES GIVE THEM VOLUME AND WEIGHT. ADD THE FINAL DETAILS, AS WELL AS THE HIGHLIGHT ON ODIE'S NOSE.

4. CLEAN UP YOUR ORIGINAL OVAL AND THE HORIZONTAL AND VERTICAL LINES. THEN FILL IN THE NOSE AND THE NECK SHADOW, AND YOU'RE DONE!

SIDE VIEW

1. TO DRAW A SIDE VIEW, CONNECT TWO OVALS FOR THE HEAD AND THE MUZZLE. THEN DRAW TWO LINES FOR THE NECK.

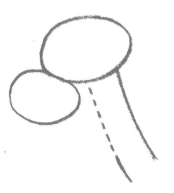

1. DRAW THE ENTIRE NECK SHAPE IN YOUR SKETCH; THEN ADD THE MOUTH AND TONGUE (WATCH OUT FOR DOG BREATH!).

2.

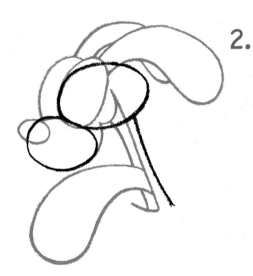

2.

3.

3.

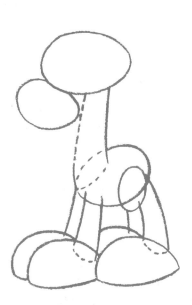

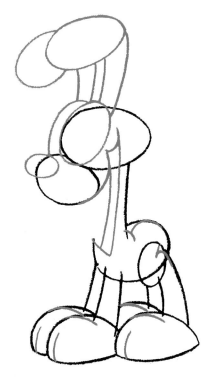

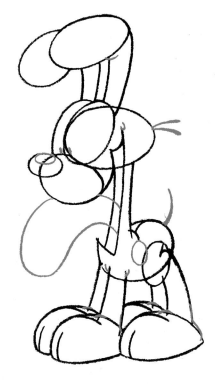

1. DRAW ODIE STANDING USING OVALS, CYLINDERS (FOR HIS NECK AND LEGS), AND HALF-CIRCLES FOR HIS FEET. THE DOTTED LINES ARE THERE IN THE SKETCH JUST TO SHOW YOU HOW THE SHAPES SHOULD FIT INTO ONE ANOTHER. THESE LINES SHOULD NOT APPEAR IN YOUR DRAWING.

2. ADD THE EARS, BRING UP THE MUZZLE LINE FOR A GREAT BIG SMILE, AND THEN ADD THE MOUTH TO THE NECK SHAPE.

3. ADD DETAILS, INCLUDING THE TAIL, THE TONGUE (DROOL IS OPTIONAL), THE HAIRS ON THE BACK OF HIS HEAD, AND THE SPOT ON HIS SIDE.

4. CLEAN UP THE SKETCH LINES WITH AN ERASER. THEN FILL IN THE BLACK AREAS AND SHADOWS.

14

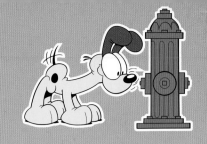

1. ODIES'S REAR LEGS LOSE THEIR TUBE SHAPE WHEN THEY ARE DRAWN UP CLOSE TO HIS BODY.

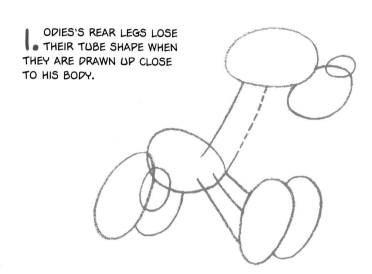

2. SWEEP THE EARS AND TONGUE BACK TO ADD THE APPEARANCE OF SPEED AND MOVEMENT TO THE DRAWING.

1. STRETCH OUT ODIE'S BODY TO MAKE HIM LOOK RELAXED.

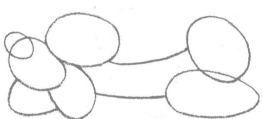

2.

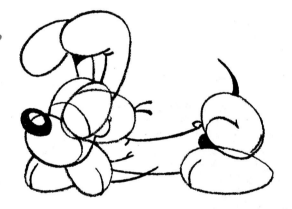

1. USE THE SAME OVAL FOR ODIE'S BODY AS IN THE SIDE VIEW, BUT THIS TIME IT SHOULD BE DRAWN BEHIND HIS NECK.

2.

3.

JON

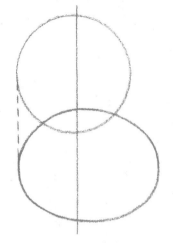

1. START BY STACKING A CIRCLE OVER AN OVAL, BUT DON'T CENTER THEM. THE DOTTED LINE SHOWS HOW TO LINE UP THESE SHAPES WHERE THEY BECOME THE BACK OF JON'S HEAD.

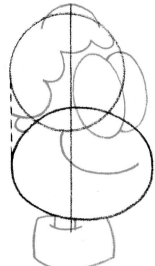

2. ADD JON'S EYES AND MOUTH AS SHOWN. THE STRAIGHT LINE DOWN THE MIDDLE IS THERE TO HELP YOU LINE UP HIS EYES, HIS NECK, AND THE TOP OF HIS HEAD.

3. JON'S HAIR IS ALWAYS MADE UP OF THE SAME AMOUNT OF BUMPS. IT WILL TAKE SOME PRACTICE TO GET THEM TO FLOW OVER THE TOP OF HIS HEAD CORRECTLY, AS SHOWN HERE.

4. FINISH YOUR DRAWING BY ADDING A FEW STRAY HAIRS AND THEN FILL IN THE SHADOWS.

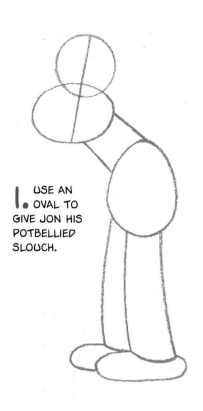

1. USE AN OVAL TO GIVE JON HIS POTBELLIED SLOUCH.

2. CONTINUE TO ADD THE DETAILS.

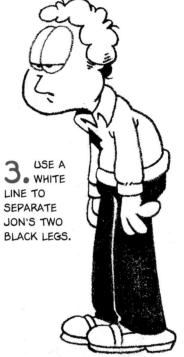

3. USE A WHITE LINE TO SEPARATE JON'S TWO BLACK LEGS.

1. TILT THE HEAD SHAPES TO GIVE THE IMPRESSION OF ACTION AND MOVEMENT.

2. DRAW JON'S LEGS TO FIT INSIDE HIS PANTS.

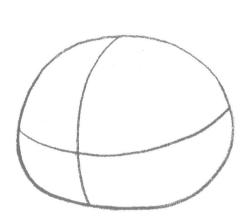

1. JUST LIKE GARFIELD, ARLENE'S HEAD STARTS WITH AN OVAL AND HORIZONTAL AND VERTICAL GUIDELINES.

2. ADD HER NOSE, EYES, EARS, AND A CURVED LINE AT THE BOTTOM OF THE OVAL FOR HER SMILE.

3. GIVE ARLENE'S HEAD A LITTLE EXTRA HEIGHT BY EXTENDING THE SIDES OF THE OVAL UP TO HER EARS. USE ANOTHER OVAL TO CREATE HER LOWER LIP.

4. FINISH HER EARS JUST LIKE GARFIELD'S AND THEN ADD ARLENE'S EYELASHES.

1.

2.

3.

THE OVAL FOR ARLENE'S BODY IS ROUGHLY HALFWAY BETWEEN HER HEAD AND FEET.

TUCK IN THE OVAL AT HER BACK SO SHE IS NOT TOO ROUND.

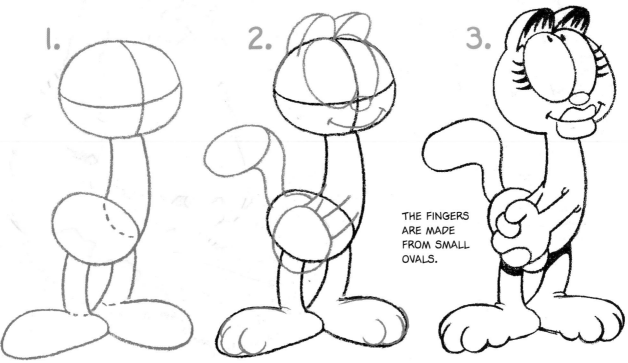

1.

2.

3.

THE FINGERS ARE MADE FROM SMALL OVALS.

POOKY

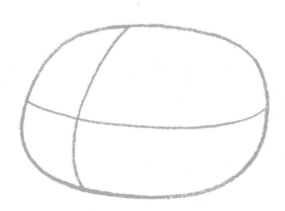

1. START WITH THE BASIC OVAL, BUT KEEP IT FLATTENED ON THE BOTTOM AS SHOWN. DRAW HORIZONTAL AND VERTICAL GUIDELINES.

2. ADD TWO DOUBLE CIRCLES TO THE TOP OF THE OVAL (THEY LOOK LIKE DOUGHNUTS, DON'T THEY?) FOR POOKY'S EARS. LEAVE SOME SPACE BETWEEN THE EARS. THE TOP OF HIS HEAD WILL GO BETWEEN THEM.

3. EXTEND THE TOP OF HIS HEAD AND HIS "HAIR." DRAW NOTCHES TO THE TOPS OF HIS EARS IN THE SHAPE OF BACKWARDS Zs.

4. COMPLETE YOUR DRAWING OF POOKY AS SHOWN. THE LINES AT THE BOTTOM OF HIS FACE SHOULDN'T ACTUALLY TOUCH.

1. POOKY IS A STUFFED TOY, SO HE DOESN'T MOVE BY HIMSELF. KEEP THAT IN MIND WHILE YOU ARE DRAWING HIM.

2. ADD SHADOWS AS SHOWN TO GIVE THE FIGURE SHAPE AND VOLUME.

3.

DEATH, TAXES

AND TEDDY BEARS

THREE THINGS YOU CAN ALWAYS COUNT ON!

JIM DAVIS 10-25

NERMAL

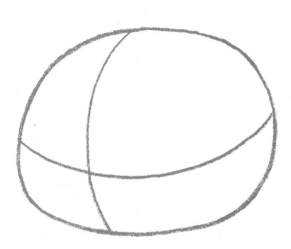

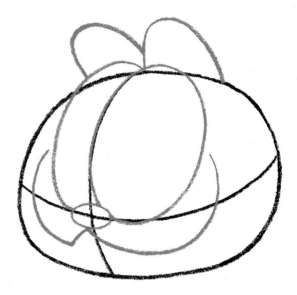

1. ONCE AGAIN, BEGIN BY DRAWING THE OVAL AND ADD LINES THAT FORM THE FRAMEWORK FOR THE HEAD.

2. POSITION NERMAL'S NOSE, EYES, EARS, AND BIG SMILE AS SHOWN.

3. NOTICE THE DIFFERENCE BETWEEN NERMAL'S EARS AND THOSE OF GARFIELD AND ARLENE.

4. THE STRIPES AND EYELASHES ARE WHAT GIVE NERMAL HIS "WORLD'S CUTEST KITTEN" LOOK. ADD THEM LAST TO COMPLETE YOUR DRAWING.

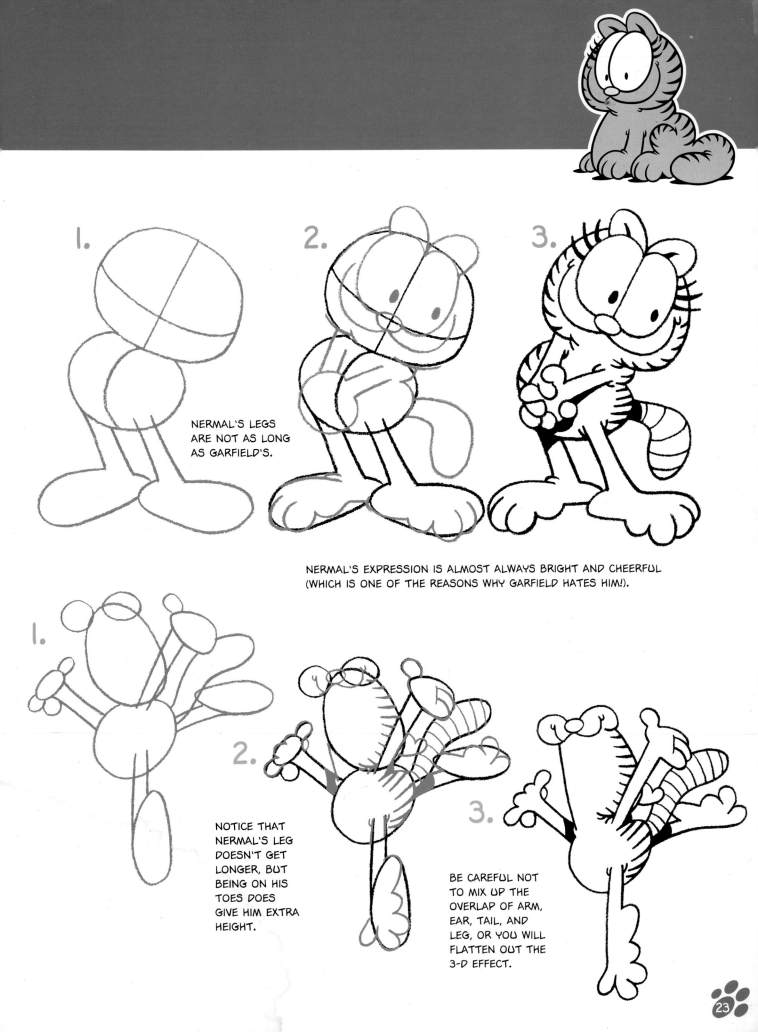

1.

NERMAL'S LEGS
ARE NOT AS LONG
AS GARFIELD'S.

2.

3.

NERMAL'S EXPRESSION IS ALMOST ALWAYS BRIGHT AND CHEERFUL
(WHICH IS ONE OF THE REASONS WHY GARFIELD HATES HIM!).

1.

2.

NOTICE THAT
NERMAL'S LEG
DOESN'T GET
LONGER, BUT
BEING ON HIS
TOES DOES
GIVE HIM EXTRA
HEIGHT.

3.

BE CAREFUL NOT
TO MIX UP THE
OVERLAP OF ARM,
EAR, TAIL, AND
LEG, OR YOU WILL
FLATTEN OUT THE
3-D EFFECT.

Here are some kooky characters to try your hand at!

GARFIELD AND
SQUEAK THE MOUSE

JON'S DAD

JON'S MOM

BINKY
THE
CLOWN

GARFIELD SAYS
THAT A DAY
WITHOUT SPIDER-
WHACKING IS LIKE
A DAY WITHOUT
PASTA.

JON'S BROTHER
DOC BOY

LIZ THE
VETERINARIAN

ACCESSORIES

CLICK
CLICK
CLICK
CLICK
CLICK

A FEW OF THE FAT CAT'S FAVORITE THINGS: A JOLTING CUP OF JAVA, A WARM BED, A FAST REMOTE CONTROL, AND A FULL FOOD DISH.

HOW THE DAILY STRIP

The Garfield comic strip appears online and in more than 2,500 newspapers around the world, making it one of the most widely read strips ever! Day in and day out, Jim Davis keeps readers laughing with the wacky adventures of Garfield, Jon, Odie, and the gang. Let's take a behind-the-scenes look at how this popular daily comic is created.

THE ROUGH SKETCH

EVERY GARFIELD COMIC STRIP BEGINS WITH A ROUGH SKETCH. THIS QUICK PENCIL DRAWING SHOWS THE CHARACTERS' EXPRESSIONS, WHAT THEY ARE DOING, AND WHERE THEY SHOULD BE PLACED WITHIN THE COMIC STRIP PANEL. THE ROUGH SKETCH ALSO INCLUDES ANY TEXT OR SOUND EFFECTS.

THE BLUE-LINE DRAWING

USING THE ROUGH SKETCH AS A GUIDE, THE STRIP IS THEN DRAWN IN BLUE PENCIL. BLUE PENCIL IS USED BECAUSE IT WILL NOT SHOW UP WHEN THE FINAL INKED VERSION IS SCANNED IN THE COMPUTER. AT THIS STAGE, THE CHARACTERS ARE DRAWN COMPLETELY, AND SCENERY OR BACKGROUND DETAILS ARE ADDED.

INKING THE STRIP

IN THE FINAL STEP, A BRUSH IS USED TO TRACE A PERMANENT BLACK LINE OVER THE BLUE PENCIL LINE. THE LETTERING IS ALSO INKED IN. THEN JIM DAVIS SIGNS AND DATES THE STRIP, AND IT'S READY TO APPEAR IN THE NEWSPAPER...BUT NOT UNTIL WEEKS—EVEN MONTHS—LATER! CARTOONISTS HAVE TO WORK AHEAD!

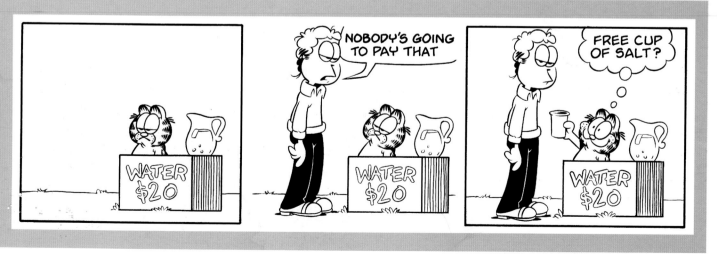

Sunday may be the day of rest, but for Garfield it's also the day of jest, and in this larger format, the fat cat can really cut loose and go crazy with more mirth, madness, and mayhem!

The Sunday strips are formatted so that they can be run by newspapers horizontally or vertically. These strips take longer to produce, so they must be created even earlier than the daily strips.

LOGO BOX
EVERY WEEK A FUN NEW LOGO BOX IS CREATED AROUND GARFIELD'S NAME.

DROP PANEL
DEPENDING ON THE WAY THE STRIP IS RUN, NEWSPAPERS HAVE THE OPTION OF OMITTING THIS PANEL, SO IT IS USUALLY A "THROWAWAY" GAG OR ACTION PANEL THAT ISN'T ESSENTIAL TO THE STRIP.

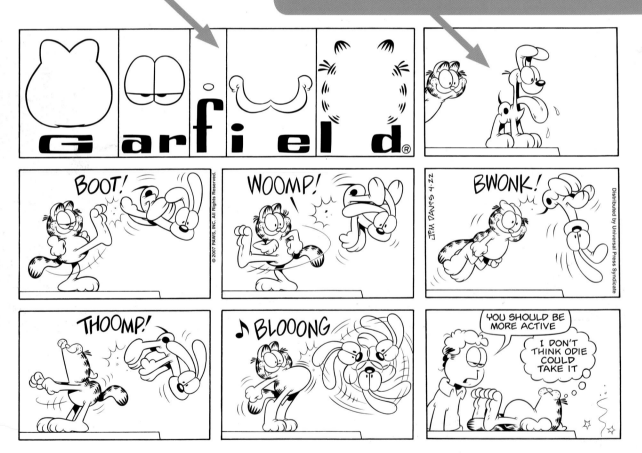

Because space in newspapers is limited, the Sunday strips have been designed so that the logo box and drop panel can be left off without affecting the comic content. When the strip appears online, however, the logo box and drop panel are never removed.

Just as in the daily strips, a rough sketch is created, followed by a blue-line drawing, and then the final inking and lettering.

After the Sunday strip is inked and lettered, it's scanned into the computer. Then, an artist adds color to the comic using a program called PhotoShop. (Fun fact: Garfield orange actually is 34% magenta and 91% yellow.) The finished piece is saved as a file and transmitted electronically to a commercial printer that creates the four-color art that will appear in the newspaper.

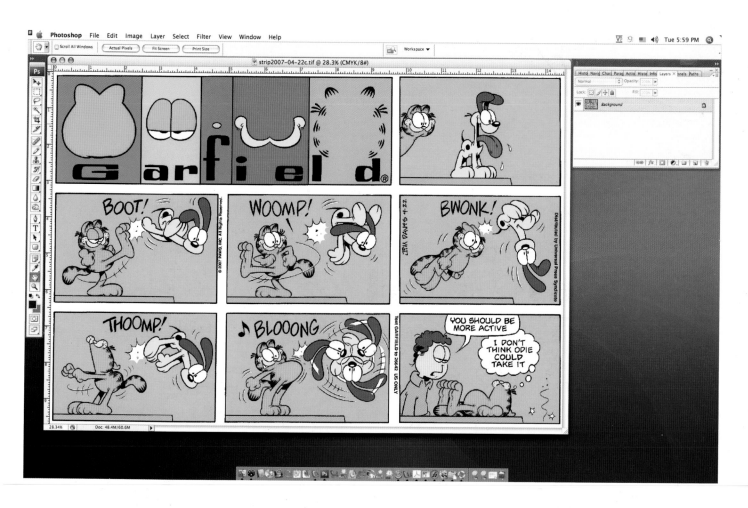

Finally, the printed Garfield comic arrives to millions of readers on Sunday morning…just in time for breakfast (do I smell bacon?).